To Auntie M

Love,

Susan.

Soul Expressions

Sacred Heart

By

Susan L

authorHOUSE™

1663 LIBERTY DRIVE, SUITE 200
BLOOMINGTON, INDIANA 47403
(800) 839-8640
WWW.AUTHORHOUSE.COM

First published by AuthorHouse 11/19/04

ISBN: 1-4208-0702-1 (sc)
ISBN: 1-4208-0703-X (dj)

Library of Congress Control Number: 2004098239

Printed in the United States of America
Bloomington, Indiana

This book is printed on acid-free paper.

A Very
Special Thanks To

Jeff & Jason Lazzari

For All
Of Their Hard Work,
Dedication And Patience,
In Creating An Extraordinary
Cover Design!

Table of Contents

Forward

I Believe

Truth Is Defined

Within Individual

Levels Of Consciousness

Within These Pages...

One Soul's Expression

"Introduction"
Word Choreographer

A writer's pencil dances
Choreographing words
Through the use of adjectives
Nouns, pronouns, and verbs

Words painting mental pictures
To help one visualize
As if they're truly seeing
Right through the author's eyes

Bringing images to life
Projecting that one cares
Exposing both, heart and soul
As each new dance is shared

A sense of obligation
Influencing each choice
Carefully considering
The power of one voice

In Loving Memory

When Dad was diagnosed
Becoming mad as hell
Venting my frustration
To God, I screamed and yelled

Three darkened days I spent
Angrily debating
Demanding higher help
Impatiently awaiting

Then my prayers were answered
With power and with might
A miracle occurred
One day, as I would write

The words began to flow
Invisible their stream
Straight through my arms and hands
Just like some crazy dream

Guiding and directing
Were Angels from above
They opened up our hearts
And healing hands of love

Family came together
To learn and understand
Energy of Reiki
And laying on of hands

Cell counts began to drop
Releasing him from pain
But didn't seem to shrink
The tumors that remained

We couldn't keep him here
Although we had believed
A miracle of Love
Is what we each received

Helping him transition
Together, his last mile
We pampered him with Love
And sent him home in style

We each said our goodbyes
While honoring his soul
Upon the wings of Angels
My Dad was carried home

Kenneth L. Carlson
Born: 7-26-1937 / Reborn: 8-1-1997

Soul Expressions

Sacred Heart

Dancing With Destiny

Buried in my heart
Sweetness of a song
Soft sounds once only whispered
Music for which I longed

Quieting the mind
Claiming inner peace
Expansion of my heart song
By volumes was increased

Lending Love the space
Inspiration flowed
Singing me a lullaby
Of wisdom my heart knows

Rescuing my life
From the hands of fate
Ever flowing streams of doubt
No longer in the way

Giving up control
Living fearlessly
Surrendering to heart songs
Dancing with destiny

Inner Child

Once upon a time
A light shined in this world
An indistinguishable
Angelic little girl

Dancing with delight
Creative and carefree
Completely limitless
In all that she could be

The inner child
Dancing in the spring
Beneath the showers
Of raindrops she would sing

Standing in her power
She knew just who she was
Connected to one source
Creator of pure Love

Couldn't have cared less
What others think or say
Strong willed and full of joy
Creating work as play

Where did she go
Who pushed her dreams away
Why is she hiding
Will she come back someday

The inner child
Sparkling she'd twirl
Her magic paintbrush
Coloring her world

Caught up in the drama
Illusions of this world
I guess I just forgot
I was that little girl

Through experience
I've learned and I have grown
Coming back full circle
To what I've long since known

I am the child
Who simply lost her way
But I've come back now
I'm coming out to play

The inner child
Dancing in the spring
Beneath the showers
Of raindrops I will sing

Mystical paint
Sparkling I twirl
My magic paintbrush
Coloring my world

Wisdom Of The Heart

Aching for truth
Unity and reconnection
Book after book
Called out to me
My mind
Thirsting endlessly
For knowledge
God
I cried
What — In those books
Was I suppose to hear?
God Answered
My child
Buying those books
You were an answer
To many
An author's prayer
I spoke to you
Not through their words
But through the silence
Between the words
Be still and know
The wisdom
Within your heart

Power Of The Mind

Imagining with innocence
It soon became quite clear
That what I'd once imagined
Through time would reappear

Though not exactly literal
Symbolic you might say
Of thoughts that I'd put out there
As words that I would pray

From parallel realities
The outcomes I received
Directly correlated
To all that I believed

Imagining deliberately
Where I had once been blind
Choosing now for higher good
The power of my mind

We Are The Angels

Drowning in illusion
Veiled, I cannot see
Struggling to remember
What's inside of me

Feeling separation
Lost and all alone
Hearing distant whispers
As soft, sweet songs from home

An Angel whispered
You're a shining star
Here to remember
Remember who you are

You can, no longer waste
Away through time and space
Confused and overwhelmed
By obstacles you face

Although sometimes afraid
I knew somehow I must
Find a way to listen
And find the strength to trust

In quiet desperation
Pretending not to hide
I took a little peek
And saw the spark inside

As this spark expanded
Glowing more and more
No longer self contained
This light then over poured

I prayed - Please lift me up
So I no longer hide
Expose to me the truth
Of who I am inside

Through my invitation
I saw once weary wings
Spreading open wide
An Angel's voice now sings

I am an Angel
I'm a shining star
And I remember
Exactly who we are

Spread now your wings
And fly with me
We are the Angels
Here – Remembering

Mastery

Higher truth
Reveals to me
Not with, but through
The eyes you see

Human mind
Knows not the soul
Clarity comes
As minds let go

Soul doth speak
Of different tongue
From long ago
When soul was young

Truth unchanged
Its rules don't bend
In beginning
Nor in the end

Masterful
Who is the soul
Whose human mind
Gives up control

To Rise Again

I AM
A beautiful
Soul
Created
In the image
And likeness
With the purity
And perfection
Of His Love
Using my gift
Of freewill choice
I've chosen
Many lifetimes
Taking myself
To the depths
Honoring
My path
Into darkness
Gaining wisdom
Through experience
Only to rise again
In truth
As the light
I AM

9

One Common Thread

Pushing my religion
I may have been deceived
Seems that I was preaching
To help "myself" believe

As I point a finger
Three fingers pointing back
Condemning another's faith
Guess who's the one in lack

Jesus or the Buddha
Debating who is Son
Keeps us separated
Not Living As The One

Only a waste of time
Upon life's precious clock
Time to be examples
It's time to walk our talk

Time for all religions
To honor – Each their own
To see one common thread
With which – All life is sewn

Loving all religions
Each truth can't be denied
Seen not as literal
Symbolically defined

So many advocators
With varying degrees
Of interpretations
And ways to be perceived

I can't quote the scriptures
Nor do I feel a need
My truth is to be lived
Not something to concede

There are so many truths
Not one is right or wrong
Based on consciousness
We are – Where we belong

Monumental beauty
A structural facade
Sewn deep within our hearts
The Living Church Of God

Be The Change

If only life
Were different
Looking outside of me
Expecting life
To change itself
To what I'd like to see
Completely
Irresponsible
Powerless to my plight
If only someone
Else would change
Then somehow – I just might
Resisting – I
Procrastinate
Until I finally see
I'm the only
Change in life
That there will be – For me
Confucius said
So long ago
That change begins within
To "BE" the change
You want to see
That's How World Change Begins

My Prayer

Please ignite the spark
Within my soul
Let my spirit speak
Of what I know
Let the voice be loud
Enough to hear
And illuminate
That which I fear
Let it clear away
This path of mine
Obstacles removed
So I may shine
Let me sing my song
Upon this world
With an opened heart
Expose my pearl
Please guide me gently
To find my place
Let me live my life
With Love and Grace

I'll Trust Myself

Leaving my past behind
I'm surrendering
Nothing left to lose
While gaining everything

I refuse to struggle
One more single day
Time to open up
Again – It's time to play

I am deliberately
Planting brand new seeds
Connecting to one source
To bring me what I need

I'll trust myself
The part of me that knows
Will find a way
Around this winding road

Right to the path
And purpose meant for me
I'll trust myself
To live truth – Joyfully

I'll no longer worry
Fearful of new things
Making space for change
Embracing what life brings

Settling no longer
Live in Joy – I must
Reclaim my self worth
With confidence and trust

From ashes I will rise
Finally to proclaim
His Holy Promise
By Living AS His Name

I'll trust myself
The part of me that knows
Will find a way
Around this winding road

Right to the path
And purpose meant for me
I'll trust myself
To live truth – Joyfully

Answers

Who am I?

Why am I here?

What's my purpose?

What should I do?

Where should I go?

Who has all the answers?

Should I?

Would I?

Could I?

What If?

. . . .

I AM

United Once Again

I see beyond, the clothes you wear
Your armored heart, your wind tossed hair
Your attitude, that you don't care
A light still shines in you

You cannot hide, for all too soon
Our world will sing, a brand new tune
As buds expose, the month of June
Life force within us all

The truth be told, you're not the flesh
There's more to you, here to express
Set free your soul, as you are blessed
With gifts you're here to share

We'll journey home, while hand in hand
Creating now, a peaceful land
Our higher self, it will command
The truth of who we are

The light in you, the light in me
Will shine as one, for all to see
The purpose is, for us to be
United Once Again

My Path

On my own agenda
Things I want to know
Goals to be achieved
Places for me to go

Then my Sacred Contracts
Consciously exposed
Who in fact's in charge
When I step out of flow

Hitting many roadblocks
Lessons were involved
Always more to learn
Some mystery to be solved

Each obstacle revealed
Answers I would need
One more puzzle piece
New truth for me to see

Random acts of chaos
Carried me along
Hand delivering
Me – Where I belonged

From a new perspective
Those roadblocks that I'd faced
Reduced to stepping stones
Paving the way to Grace

Flowing from the inside
Then straightened out my path
More peaceful and serene
Looking back – I laugh

Letting go of outcomes
Of my expectations
Living for the journey
Not the destination

Shadow Dancing

Born into this world
A spark of the Divine
It was my intention
To live God's Will as mine

But – Using my freewill
Shadow dancing I would go
Caught in the illusion
Forgetting what I know

Drowning in my darkness
Heart bitter and so tough
Dropping to my knees
I plea – I've had enough

Without any judgment
Guided from above
My spirit lifted up
Through unconditional Love

My heart now holds the truth
Compassion I have learned
For those still shadow dancing
The Flame Of Hope – I Burn

20

Time Shift

Mysterious
This dream of mine
Channeling words
Brought through in rhyme
Their purpose is
To somehow change
The minds of man
To rearrange
Through freewill choice
We've run a muck
For centuries
Becoming stuck
Provoking thought
New points of view
Unraveling
To bring in new
We're shifting now
Perceptions of
Intolerance
Back into Love

Happily Ever After

Half my life I felt
As empty as could be
Something wasn't right
Deep inside of me

As to be searching
Throughout all time and space
For my other half
To fill that empty place

That special someone
For more than just awhile
Who would complete me
And always make me smile

True Love fulfilling
One Love eternally
My own prince charming
Who'd come and rescue me

My own fairy tale
In happiness would end
With the realization
Of where it all began

I'd disconnected
Myself from source above
Which separated
Myself – From my own Love

Honoring myself
Embracing shadow parts
While reconnecting
Has filled my empty heart

My search has ended
In search of Love no more
I am the true Love
That I'd been searching for

Never Too Late

I Dream

Of A World

Free From Hate

With

Abundance

Peace And Love

A Miracle

Most Possible

As One

With God Above

Earth Angel

Many Angels walk this Earth
Within the human form
Effecting countless others
With presence that transforms

One Angel's name is Oprah
Serving humanity
With such illumination
One cannot help but see

Her beauty is reflective
Shining as our mirror
Helping us to see ourselves
Not simply to endear

She's taken her rightful place
Upon her jeweled thrown
Not for us to admire – But
To get up on our own

Standing with integrity
Living her highest truth
The greatest of examples
We should aspire to

Humble yet empowering
Preacher of strong self worth
One of THE most powerful
Angels Upon This Earth

Playing The Victim Game

I came to play the victim
Abused as little girl
I held on to resentment
Which shaped my inner world

Within I formed a pattern
Which drew experience
Troubled relationships
Which now – Make perfect sense

I'd come to change this pattern
The choice was always mine
Every opportunity
Within my own time line

I'd given up my power
And was the one to blame
For later circumstances
Playing the victim game

Mirroring, back to myself
My own deep inner pain
Until I quit Re-Acting
A victim — I'd remain

Finally forgiving my past
Compassion then would start
Releasing heavy burdens
I'd carried in my heart

No longer playing the roll
Of victim — As before
Brand new opportunities
Came knocking at my door

Enjoying new found freedom
Is awe inspiring
Creating a life of joy
Within — My heart now sings

Full Circle

Breathtaking vision
Majestic Mother Earth
Land of freewill choice
Duality was birthed

Temporarily
Forgetting what we know
As amnesiacs
And walking comatose

Fulfillment of the plan
The reason for our birth
Human Evolution
Transforming planet Earth

We've sunken to the depths
As far as we can go
Coming back full circle
Awakened – We will know

A New World

Sensing transformation
Ascension if you will
Raising our vibration
Soul's vision is fulfilled

Awakened to much more
Than visually exists
Feeling now quite clearly
Multidimensional mists

Others are assisting
Although we cannot see
Gently we are lifted
To be all we can be

A thought transference here
Synchronicity there
Transforming duality
Shifting from this nightmare

Messages from heaven
Come streaming through my mind
Faint memories held dear
A long – Lost place in time

Pulling from parallels
Simultaneously
We are recreating
A New World – To Be Seen

Mystery School

Incinerate

Old textbook rules

All incompetent

Teaching tools

It matters not

What authors say

Each one will learn

In unique ways

No manuals

One set of rules

Soul's teaching comes

Through mystery schools

The Kingdom Within

Bringing focus
Into your heart
Bypassing intellect

Awakening
To higher truth
Each time you reconnect

The little you
Soon steps aside
Your higher self steps through

Greater wisdom
Magnifying
A purpose meant for you

All needs fulfilled
Quite naturally
As your new flow begins

Because your choice
Was seeking first
The Kingdom From Within

Unlimited

If:
Life Is An Illusion
We Create
Our Own Reality
As I Am – So Shall It Be
Pretend – Means – Pre Intention
There Is A Law Of Cause And Effect
To Believe Is To Receive
We Reap What We Sow
Etc., Etc., Etc.

Then:
What's Our Problem
We're Unlimited
Let's
DREAM BIG
And
FAKE IT
TILL WE MAKE IT !

Passion

Like an orange being squeezed
Produces orange juice
Put under any pressure
What's in – Comes out of you

It's time to start transforming
Illusions held inside
And fuel your inner passion
Where spirit still abides

Creating inspiration
Peace and serenity
Connected to your Life Force
Supportive energy

For leisure, life, and Love
Passion changes everything
Intensifying feelings
With Joy – A Spirit Sings

It doesn't really matter
Whatever you aspire
Set free your inner passion
Fulfilling Hearts Desire

Here To Win

In a Win – Win
Situation
We'll see how WE create
No more separation
Prejudice or hate

In a Win – Win
Situation
There's no more pain and strife
Living celebration
Honoring all life

In a Win – Win
Situation
We'll all be letting go
Joy and jubilation
Joining in one flow

In a Win – Win
Situation
We're laying down our swords
Free from confrontation
Peace - As Our Reward

In This Moment

In this moment
I put my past behind
To Re-create
A shift to higher mind

In this moment
With energy divine
A brand new life
Can easily be mine

In this moment
Blank canvases appear
Painting pictures
Of what my heart holds dear

In this moment
I plant those pictures deep
And letting go
Trust – nurturing those seeds

In this moment
All dreams I can conceive
Will manifest
If Only I Believe

As I Am

As I journey through this life
Behold – What do I see
Only a reflection
Of what's inside of me

Expressing thought, word and deed
One truth – It does decree
Coming back full circle
Only what I've conceived

As I embrace higher truth
Spreading universally
One Love – Within us all
Expands to be received

Hearts full of Peace, Love and Joy
Shine through – Illumining
And energetically
It changes everything

One spirit in expression
Influencing the All
Raising soul's vibration
More clearly to recall

As Creator – Just One Source
I AM – Can't help but BE
While we're standing – Face to face
I AM – Looks back at me

Remembering who we are
I AM – Powerful indeed
Without limitation
Manifesting my own dreams

So shall it be – So shall it be
That I create the world I see
Manifesting change – Comes naturally
When I Realize

As I Am – So Shall It Be

Love

Love Is Pure
Love Is Constant
Love … Just … IS
Anger – Is Not Love
And Yet – It Allows Us
To Feel The Difference
There Is Love – Or – There Is Not
We Are It – Or – Fall From It
Each Pivotal Moment
WE FEEL
What Love Is
Or Is Not
Allowing Us
An Opportunity
TO CHOOSE…
When Every
Thought, Word
And Deed
Expresses Love
Unceasingly
WE'LL ♥ "BE" ♥ LOVE

As Butterflies

Like caterpillars
We roam the Earth
Searching respite
To be Re-birthed

A sacred journey
In silk surround
Safely protected
Far from the ground

In simple solace
We nestle in
Through self reflection
New life begins

Briefly detained in
Incubation
Preparing for our
Transformation

Spreading our wings of
Radiant light
As Butterflies
We then take flight

Thy Will Be Done

Here – Within this lifetime
The battle has begun
We're all rectifying
The truth of what we've done

Through complete surrender
Thy will be done – Not mine
Being Accountable
For plans of the Divine

Shadows will be dissolved
Giving up their power
Within the light of Love
They'll see their final hour

Through complete acceptance
No judgment or distain
Emitting only light
No darkness shall remain

Darkness cannot exist
Illumined in the light
Penetrating darkness
With Love's pure power and might

The healing of the world
Brought through simplicity
Living Heaven On Earth
God's Plan Will Come To Be

Controversial

Actions
Not Words
Speak Truth…
Who
In Truth
"Is" Christian?
Who Is
A Living
Breathing
"Example"
Of The Christ
Principle?
How Do I Judge Thee?
Let Me Count The Ways…
Courageous Few
Will Live
From Within
Reaching Perfection
The Rest Of US
Resume
To Pre-Tend

No More Willy Nilly

Becoming caught up in
The drama of my life
I'd made it my life's mission
To live in pain and strife

Deciding then to change
The patterns of my past
Creating with the future
Pure joy will reign at last

Though shadows reappeared
With nowhere else to hide
Viewing aspects of myself
I'd smile and step aside

Hell's fury rising up
For all that it was worth
For I had chosen Heaven
While living on this Earth

Stepping out of darkness
And responsibly
Living life outside the box
Setting myself free

Trust then opened doorways
I never knew were there
Now, I'm enjoying freedom
A path once only dared

Totally accepting
Of other's freewill choice
Teaching through example
Example as my voice

Now that I remember
Why I came to this Earth
Ending my sins of judgment
A new world will be birthed

No more willy nilly
No more dark night of soul
I'm living life on purpose
I'm living life as whole

No more willy nilly
I am deliberate
Creating with a passion
The life for which I'm meant

Forever Love

Forever Love
Shining a new
Will lift us up
To see us through
When we are lost
It lights the way
Providing strength
Through darkened days

Forever Love
Dawns from one source
When hence chosen
Sails steer our course
Its gentleness
Fills empty space
A soft cocoon
Its warm embrace

Forever Love
Our Only Saving Grace

Through God's Eyes

How could your perception
Be so far from the truth
Illusions of yourself
Distort your point of view

I wish that you could see
One moment through my eyes
To erase the damage
Of self inflicted lies

While seeing through my eyes
You'd see yourself as light
Ethereal beauty
Surrounds you day and night

Being near you warms my heart
Your presence emanates
A love so warm and pure
Why is it you – you hate

If you could only see
One moment through my eyes
Seeing inner beauty
Transcending shape or size

There are so many reasons
I have for loving you
I wish that you could Love
Yourself – The Way I Do !

Strong On My Own

I gave my heart
And soul away
Then over time
I lost my way

There's no one else
But me – To blame
For twenty years
I played his game

With his new blonde
He let us go
The timing was
For me to grow

No more giving
Myself away
To anyone
In any way

A pattern that
I must admit
Was lived out for
My benefit

With self respect
I won't repeat
What I allowed
To destroy me

Forgiving him
Then set me free
Restoring power
Belonged to me

A new program
Now fuels my soul
I am myself
Complete and whole

No longer lost
Strong on my own
More powerful
Because I've grown

I'm grateful now
He chose to leave
The gift was mine
I Do Believe

You're Not Alone

I Haven't Left

I'm Here With You

You're Not Alone

I'll See You Through

I Stand With You

You Stand With Me

We Stand As One

Through All Eternity

One Among The Angels

Standing in your shadow
Should you happen to fall

Forever there to guide you
At your beckon call

No earthly body living
Eternal lives the soul

Healthy, happy, loving
With God – Forever whole

Fear not – The great unknown
In time we all shall see

Residing in the heavens
All live eternally

No more pain and suffering
No more sacrifice

One among the Angels
Back home in paradise

As Artist

If Life
It Were
A Canvas
And I
Its Paint
And Brush
As Artist
I'd Create
All Vegetation
Lush
Abundantly
Producing
Shared
With One
And All
Ending
World Hunger
Heeding
Spirit's Call

Guardian Angel

As I wander through each new day
Content as I can be
I have a wonderful feeling
Someone is watching me

I have a guardian Angel
An Angel I can't see
I have a guardian Angel
Who's watching over me

When faced with a tough decision
I let my mind be still
And ask my guardian Angel
To guide me, if she will

Some may say it's their conscience
That guides them through each day
But, I have a guardian Angel
Who's showing me the way

Message To Myself

Achieve
True
And Lasting
Change
Willingly
Embracing
The Unknown
Accepting
Unfamiliar
Discomfort
Stepping Outside
The Proverbial Box
Of Claustrophobic
Stagnation
Taking A Leap
Experiencing Life
Through New Eyes
A Courageous Heart
And – An Open Mind

Sacred Heart

Each journey ours
Each one unique
And for ourselves
To be critiqued
Priorities
To rearrange
With freewill choice
For growth and change
Our consciousness
Once shifted slow
To realign
To truth we know
Acceleration
Is soon to start
Self – Realized
The Sacred Heart
Awake again
We journey home
To Re-Unite
Ourselves – As One

Mystery Solved

The same old song
And dance routine
Will play no more
Dramatic scenes

Holographs
Will change my theme
To manifest
Much higher dreams

The veil will lift
For me to see
Both where I've been
And where I'll be

Though I've enjoyed
Whirling through time
Circle's complete
On this time line

Creating with
New energy
A brand new world
For me to see

As I'm shifting
My sleep will end
And consciously
I will ascend

Centered within
Complete and whole
Returned to joy
I'll be at home

Living as Love
My soul evolved
My task complete
The mystery solved

False Prophet Within

My ego
Is an accumulation
Of false data
Experiences
And beliefs
Recorded within
My human
Cellular structure
Some beliefs
Built solely on
Another's perception
Forced upon me
And accepted
By me
In my weakened
Energetic state
Standing strong
In my power
Fully connected
To Source
No false prophecy
Shall remain

Soul Set Free

When someone dies
I feel such joy
And No – I'm not that nuts
As I express
This – As my truth
I know it takes some guts
But – What I feel
As one goes home
Is how I think they're met
Purely joyous
Celebration
For time on Earth they've spent
Along with joy
I must admit
A little jealously
For they've gone home
And here I am
In body – physically
Feeling selfish
When I cry
Tears falling just for me
Because I know
They are not sad
Their soul has been set free

Heart Break

When a heart
Breaks open
We quickly
Try to mend
By closing it
Back up
To bring pain
To an end
BUT HEARTS ♥ BREAK ♥ FOR A REASON
Allowed
To open wide
Creates
A larger space
Where God's Love
Still abides
Expansion
Of one's heart
Will mend it
Naturally
Once larger
Than before
More Love
Shall Be Received

The Return

Many Await
The Return
Of Christ
And – Indeed
WE ARE
Returning
"CHRIST"
OUR ETERNAL ☼ FLAME ☼ IS WITHIN US
And Will
Return
As Each
One Of Us
Allows
Ourselves
To Stand
In The Light
Of Truth
And Emerge
AS WHO
WE ARE
One Light
One Love
One Truth
In Many
Disguises

Revelations

Consciousness is shifting
Here in our final years
Effects will be revealed
Of our projected fears

Mirrors will appear
Shadows for us to face
Of all that we're inflicting
Upon the human race

Over zealous egos
Shrinking to rightful size
Spirit is expanding
Before our very eyes

We cannot separate
The church from any state
Because WE ARE the church
And waste time in debate

Not "Being" who we are
Just negates our power
Creating our demise
Our crumbling ivory tower

Upheaval from within
Not retaliation
Living the prophecy
Times of Revelation

Self evaluating
We're cleaning up this mess
Responsibility
"Being" - Our final test

Facing our own judgments
A gift we have received
To end our sinful ways
Three Thousand Years Of Peace

Empowered Once Again

What's done is done
Left far behind
Hearts will open
To changing humankind

New sun will rise
For all to see
Shedding new light
Changing history

We will not give
Ourselves away
Show disrespect
Or join in ego play

A time to share
One Sacred Love
With dignity
We're all deserving of

New sun will rise
For all to see
Shedding new light
New opportunity

Our hearts fulfilled
Complete as one
Within ourselves
There comes a rising sun

Returned to peace
Self worth regained
Compassion learned
Heaven on Earth retained

The past behind
Our joy begins
Love's creation
Empowered once again

If You Only Knew

If you only knew
Who walked with you
You'd shed your final tear
In a faithful way
Loving each day
Laughing away all fear

If you only knew
Who walked with you
Down each and every mile
You'd never look back
Your mind relaxed
Wearing a great big smile

If you only knew
Who walked with you
All burdens you'd release
Just being the star
You truly are
Living God's Gift Of Peace

About The Author

Embracing who I am
Single Mother of three
Raising three young men
As my life's destiny

Flaunting no PHD
Living my own devise
Makes me qualified
To give no one advise

The wisdom that I share
Not to show that I'm smart
Just experienced
To share what's in my heart

Living in gratitude
Approval – I don't seek
Perfectly content
To Let My Spirit Speak

Section II

In these final pages
Another Dream Of Mine
Hearing words someday
As lyrics down the line

Verses are repeated
Words slightly modified
Creating Heart Songs
When music is applied

As these Soul Expressions
Evolve to something new
Soon – It is my hope
These songs are shared with you

Soul
Expressions

"Heart Songs"

We Are The Angels

Drowning in illusion
Veiled – I cannot see
Struggling to remember
What's inside of me
Feeling separation
Lost and all alone
Hearing distant whispers
As soft, sweet songs from home

CHORUS:
An Angel whispered
You're a shining star
Here to remember
Remember who you are

Set free your soul
No longer will you hide
Release the Angel
You know you are inside

No longer can I waste
Away through time and space
Confused and overwhelmed
By obstacles I face
Maybe I'll be afraid
But know – somehow I must
Find a way to listen
And find the strength to trust

CHORUS:
Again – an Angel whispered
You're a shining star
Here to remember
Remember who you are

Set free your soul
No longer will you hide
Release the Angel
You know you are inside

In quiet desperation
Pretending not to hide
I took a little peek
And saw the spark inside

As this spark expanded
Glowing more and more
No longer self contained
This light – then over poured

CHORUS:
Hesitant – I whispered
I'm a shining star
Here to remember
Remember who we are

Set free my soul
I don't want to hide
Release the Angel
I know – I am inside

69

I prayed please lift me up
So – I no longer hide
Expose to me the truth
Of who I am inside
Through my invitation
I saw – Once weary wings
Spreading open wide
An Angel's voice now sings

CHORUS:
I am an Angel
I'm a shining star
Here to remember
Remember – who we are

Setting free my soul
I no longer hide
I released the Angel
The one – I am inside

I am an Angel
I'm a shining star
And I remember
Exactly who we are

Set free your soul
And fly with me
We are the Angels
Here – Remembering

You're Not Alone

Standing in your shadow
Should you happen to fall
Forever there to guide you
At your beckon call
  CHORUS:
  I haven't left
  I'm here with you
  You're not alone
  I'll see you through
  I stand with you
  You stand with me
  We stand as one
  Through all eternity

No earthly body living
Eternal lives the soul
Healthy, happy, loving
With God – Forever whole
  CHORUS: (Repeated)

Fear not the great unknown
In time we all shall see
Residing in the heavens
All live – Eternally
  CHORUS: (Repeated)

No more pain and suffering
No more sacrifice
One among the Angels
Back home in paradise
  CHORUS: (Repeated)

Shadow Dancing

Born into this world
A spark of the Divine
It was my intention
To live God's will as mine
But using my freewill
Shadow dancing I would go
Caught in the illusion
Forgetting what I know

CHORUS:
I went shadow dancing
Forgetting who I am
I went shadow dancing
The path for which I came
No lesser was His Love
His spark – It burns in me
Allowed my choice to suffer
Never once – Did He leave me

Drowning in my darkness
Heart bitter and so tough
Dropping to my knees
I plea – I've had enough

CHORUS:
I'd gone shadow dancing
Forgetting who I am
I'd gone shadow dancing
The path for which I came
No lesser was His Love
His spark it burns in me
Allowed my choice to suffer
Never once – Did He leave me

Without any judgment
Guided from above
My spirit lifted up
Through unconditional Love
CHORUS:
No longer shadow dancing
Exploring who I am
No longer shadow dancing
The path for which I came
Love turned up the light
And fueled the flame in me
Surrendering my will
Setting my soul free

Born into this world
A spark of the Divine
Spreading hope and joy
I chose God's will as mine
My heart now holds the truth
Compassion I have learned
For those still shadow dancing
The flame of hope – I burn

CHORUS:
No longer shadow dancing
I know who I am
No longer shadow dancing
The path for which I came
Love turned up the light
And fueled the flame in me
For other shadow dancers
The flame of hope – I'll be

CHORUS: (Repeated)

Dancing With Destiny

Buried in my heart
Sweetness of a song
Soft sounds – once only whispered
Music for which I longed

CHORUS:
I longed to dance
Dance with destiny
Flowing as the river
Creating my soul's dreams
I longed to dance
To dance with destiny

Quieting the mind
Claiming inner peace
Expansion of my heart song
By volumes – was increased
Lending Love the space
Inspiration flowed
Singing me a lullaby
Of wisdom – my heart knows

CHORUS:
I am now light
And feel so free
There's so much joy
Inside of me
It seems as though
I'm dancing with destiny

Rescuing my life
From the hands of fate
Ever flowing streams of doubt
No longer in the way

CHORUS:
Now – I am dancing
Dancing with destiny
Flowing as the river
Creating my soul's dreams
I'm interactively
Dancing with destiny

Giving up control
Living fearlessly
Surrendering to heart songs
Dancing with destiny

CHORUS:
I am now light
And feel so free
There's so much joy
Inside of me
I can't believe
I've fulfilled my dream
Of dancing with destiny

Now – I am dancing
Dancing with destiny
Flowing as the river
Creating my soul's dreams
I'm – Interactively
Dancing with destiny

One Heart – One Soul

I see beyond
The clothes you wear
Your armored heart
Your wind tossed hair
Your attitude
That you don't care
A light still shines in you

CHORUS:
One heart – one mind
One heart – one soul
One light that shines
Within us all
Remembering
Forever whole
As one – We're going home

You cannot hide
For all too soon
Our world will sing
A brand new tune
As buds expose
The month of June
Life force within us all

CHORUS: (Repeated)

The truth be told
You're not the flesh
There's more to you
Here to express
Set free your soul
As you are blessed
With gifts – You're here to share

CHORUS: (Repeated)

We'll journey home
While hand in hand
Creating now
A peaceful land
Our higher self
It will command
The truth of who we are

CHORUS: (Repeated)

The light in you
The light in me
Will shine as one
For all to see
The purpose is
For us to be
United – Once again

CHORUS: (Repeated twice)

As I Am

As I journey through this life
Behold – What do I see
Only a reflection
Of what's inside of me

Expressing thought, word, and deed
One truth – It does decree
Coming back full circle
Only what I've conceived

CHORUS:
So shall it be – So shall it be
That I create – The world I see
Manifesting change
Comes naturally
When I realize
As I Am – So shall it be

As I embrace higher truth
Spreading Universally
One love within us all
Expands to be received

Hearts full of peace, love and joy
Shine through – Illumining

And energetically
It changes everything

CHORUS: (Repeated)

One spirit in expression
Influencing the All
Raising soul's vibration
More clearly to recall

As creator – Just one source
I AM – Can't help – But BE
While we're standing face to face
I AM – Looks back at me

CHORUS: (Repeated)

Remembering – Who we are
I AM – Powerful indeed
Without limitations
Manifesting my own dreams

CHORUS: (Repeated)

So shall it be – So shall it be
That I create – The world I see
Manifesting change – Comes naturally
When I Realize
As I AM – So Shall it be

Inner Child

Once upon a time
A light shined in this world
An indistinguishable
Angelic little girl
Dancing with delight
Creative and carefree
Completely limitless
In all that she could be

CHORUS:
Where did she go
Who pushed her dreams away
Why is she hiding
Will she come back someday
The inner child
Dancing in the spring
Beneath the showers
Of raindrops she would sing
Mystical paint
Sparkling she'd twirl
Her magic paintbrush
Coloring her world

Standing in her power
She knew just who she was
Connected to one source
Creator of pure love
Couldn't have cared less
What others think or say
Strong willed and full of joy
Creating work – As play

Caught up in the drama
Illusions of this world
I guess I just forgot
I was that little girl
Through experience
I've learned and I have grown
Coming back full circle
To what I've long since known

CHORUS:
I am the child
Who simply lost her way
But I've come back now
I'm coming out to play

The inner child
Dancing in the spring
Beneath the showers
Of raindrops I will sing

Mystical paint
Sparkling I twirl
My magic paintbrush
Coloring my world

I am the child
Dancing in the spring
Beneath the showers
Of raindrops I will sing

Mystical paint
Sparkling I twirl
My magic paintbrush
Coloring my world

No More Willy Nilly

Becoming caught up in
The drama of my life
I'd made it my life's mission
To live in pain and strife
Deciding then to change
The patterns of my past
Creating with the future
Pure joy will reign at last

CHORUS:
No more willy nilly
No more dark night of soul
I'm living life on purpose
I'm living life as whole
No more willy nilly
I am deliberate
Creating with a passion
The life for which I'm meant

Though shadows reappeared
With nowhere else to hide
Viewing aspects of myself
I'd smile and step aside
Hell's fury rising up
For all that it was worth
For I had chosen heaven
While living on this earth

CHORUS: (Repeated)

82

Stepping out of darkness
And responsibly
Living life outside the box
Setting myself free
Trust then opened doorways
I never knew were there
Now – I'm enjoying freedom
A path – Once only dared

CHORUS: (Repeated)

Totally accepting
Of other's freewill choice
Teaching through example
Example as my voice
Now that I remember
Why I came to this earth
Ending my sins of judgment
A new world will be birthed

CHORUS:
No more willy nilly
No more dark night of soul
I'm living life on purpose
I'm living life as whole
No more willy nilly
I am deliberate
Creating with a passion
The life for which I'm meant
No more willy nilly
I am deliberate
Creating with a passion
The life for which I'm meant

Empowered Once Again

What's done is done
Left far behind
Hearts will open
To changing humankind
CHORUS:
New sun will rise
For all to see
Shedding new light
Changing history

We will not give
Ourselves away
Show disrespect
Or join in ego play
CHORUS:
New sun will rise
For all to see
Shedding new light
New opportunity

A time to share
One Sacred Love
With dignity
We're all deserving of
CHORUS:
New sun will rise
For all to see
Shedding new light
Changing history
The past behind
Our joy begins
Love's creation
Empowered once again

Our hearts fulfilled
Complete as one
Within ourselves
There comes a rising sun
CHORUS:
New sun will rise
For all to see
Shedding new light
New opportunity
The past behind
Our joy begins
Love's creation
Empowered once again

Returned to peace
Self worth regained
Compassion learned
Heaven on Earth retained
CHORUS:
New sun will rise
For all to see
Shedding new light
New opportunity
The past behind
Our joy begins
Love's creation
Empowered once again
The past behind
Our joy begins
Love's creation
Empowered once again

Forever Love

Sensing transformation
Ascension if you will
Raising our vibration
Soul's vision is fulfilled
Awakened to much more
Than visually exists
Feeling now quite clearly
Multidimensional mists

CHORUS:
Forever Love
Shining a new
Will lift us up
To see us through
When we are lost
It lights the way
Providing strength
Through darkened days

Others are assisting
Although we cannot see
Gently we are lifted
To be all we can be
A thought transference here
Synchronicity there
Transforming duality
Shifting from this nightmare

CHORUS:
Forever Love
Dawns from one source
When hence chosen
Sails steer our course
Its gentleness
Fills empty space
A soft cocoon
Its warm embrace

Messages from Heaven
Come streaming through my mind
Faint memories held dear
A long – Lost place in time
Pulling from parallels
Simultaneously
We are recreating
A new world to be seen

CHORUS:
Forever Love
Shining a new
Will lift us up
To see us through
When we are lost
It lights the way
Providing strength
Through darkened days
Its gentleness
Fills empty space
A soft cocoon
Its warm embrace

Forever Love – Our Only Saving Grace

Soul Of Mastery

Higher truth
Reveals to me
Not with – But through
The eyes you see

CHORUS:
There's higher truth
We all know of
Heard in the void
Sent from above
So listen now
And you will see
You are a soul
Of mastery

Human mind
Knows – Not the soul
Clarity comes
As minds let go
Soul doth speak
Of different tongue
From long ago
When soul was young

CHORUS: *(Repeated)*

Truth unchanged
Its rules don't bend
In beginning
Nor – In the end
Masterful
Who is the soul
Whose human mind
Gives up control

CHORUS:
There's higher truth
We all know of
Heard in the void
Sent from above
So listen now
And you will see
You are a soul
Of mastery

Yes listen now
And you will see
You are a soul
Of mastery

I'll Trust Myself

Leaving my past behind
I'm surrendering
Nothing left to lose
While gaining everything

I refuse to struggle
One more single day
Time to open up
Again – It's time to play

CHORUS:
I'll trust myself
The part of me that knows
Will find a way
Around this winding road
Right to the path
And purpose meant for me
I'll trust myself
To live truth – Joyfully

I am deliberately
Planting brand new seeds
Connecting to one source
To bring me what I need
I'll no longer worry
Fearful of new things
Making space for change
Embracing what life brings

CHORUS: (Repeated)

Settling – No longer
Live in Joy – I must
Reclaim my self worth
With confidence and trust

From ashes – I will rise
Finally to proclaim
His Holy Promise
By Living AS His Name

CHORUS: (Repeated Twice)

Thank You

I hope that you've enjoyed
The sharing of one soul
Essence through this vessel
As Susan – I am known

Though never truly separate
From anybody else
Only in perception
Expressing as myself

I pray you'll find the gift
Of living Love with ease
For through – Our state of "Being"
World Peace Will Be Achieved

God Bless !!!

Visit

TrineDesigns.Com
For Gifts Of
Inspiration & Empowerment

From the author of
Soul Expressions

About The Author

Embracing her life as the single mother of three young men, the author of "Soul Expressions" has opened her heart to share her journey of self realization, through her soul expressed, condensed messages: Including - Who we are, Why we're here, and What our purpose is, As we journey through this life as...

Spiritual Beings - Living The Human Experience!

9 781420 807035